# Suzuki®

## BASS SCHOOL

Volume 1
Bass Part
*Revised Edition*

AMPV: 1.01

Available in the following formats: Book (0370S), Book & CD Kit (40727), CD (0369)

Book
ISBN-10: 0-7390-5175-X
ISBN-13: 978-0-7390-5175-7

Book & CD Kit
ISBN-10: 0-7390-9713-X
ISBN-13: 978-0-7390-9713-7

# FOREWORD

This volume of Suzuki Bass School is the product of years of research conducted by various double bass teachers of the Suzuki Association of the Americas.

In the past few decades, a significant number of teachers of young bassists have chosen to initiate left-hand instruction at the neck block. Many other teachers prefer the more traditional method of beginning instruction at the first position. This revised version of Suzuki Bass School, Volume 1, is designed to accommodate both approaches.

The optional repertoire marked A-F is presented for those who wish to begin the left-hand pedagogy at the neck block. For those who prefer the traditional approach and for those who have completed the optional unit, instruction should begin or continue with the "Twinkle Variations" in first position.

— The Bass Committee of the Suzuki Association of the Americas

# INTRODUCTION

*FOR THE STUDENT:* This material is part of the worldwide Suzuki Method® of teaching. The companion recording should be used along with this publication. A piano accompaniment book is also available for this material.

*FOR THE TEACHER:* In order to be an effective Suzuki teacher, ongoing education is encouraged. Each regional Suzuki association provides teacher development for its membership via conferences, institutes, short-term and long-term programs. In order to remain current, you are encouraged to become a member of your regional Suzuki association, and if not already included, the International Suzuki Association.

*FOR THE PARENT:* Credentials are essential for any teacher you choose. We recommend you ask your teacher for his or her credentials, especially those relating to training in the Suzuki Method®. The Suzuki Method® experience should foster a positive relationship among the teacher, parent and child. Choosing the right teacher is of the utmost importance.

To obtain more information about the Suzuki Association in your region, please contact:

International Suzuki Association
www.internationalsuzuki.org

# CONTENTS

# A
# Twinkle, Twinkle, Little Star Variations

S. Suzuki

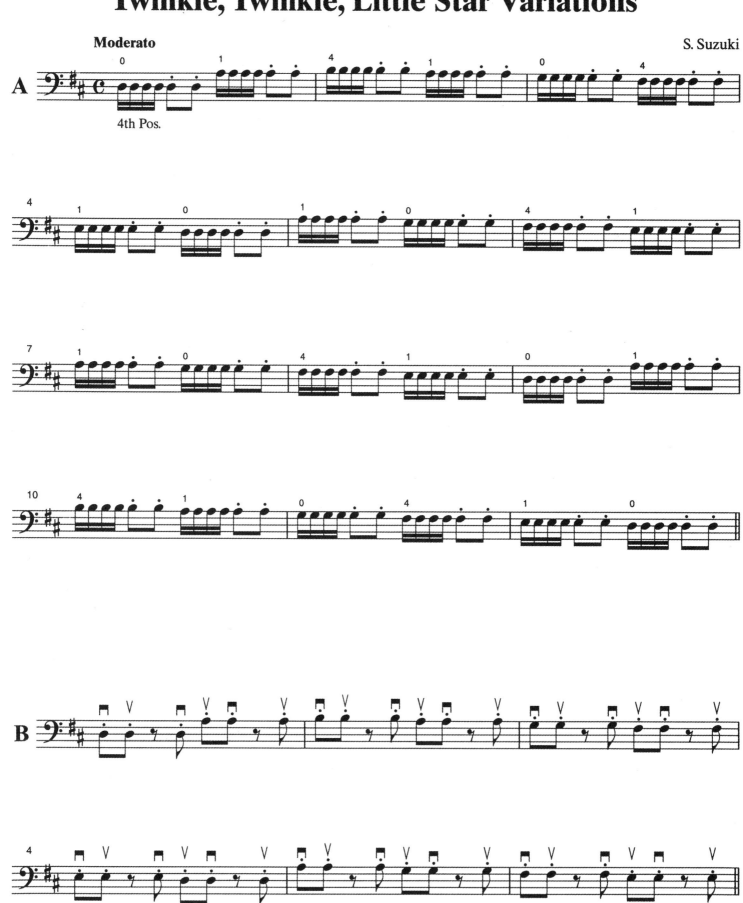

**C**

etc.

**D**

etc.

**E**

etc.

# Theme

# B
# Go Tell Aunt Rhody

Folk Song

# C
# Lightly Row

Folk Song

# Tonalization

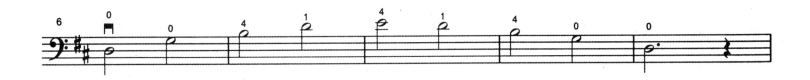

# D
# Song of the Wind

# E
# May Song

**Allegro moderato**

Folk Song

# F
# O Come, Little Children

Folk Song

# 1
# Twinkle, Twinkle, Little Star Variations

S. Suzuki

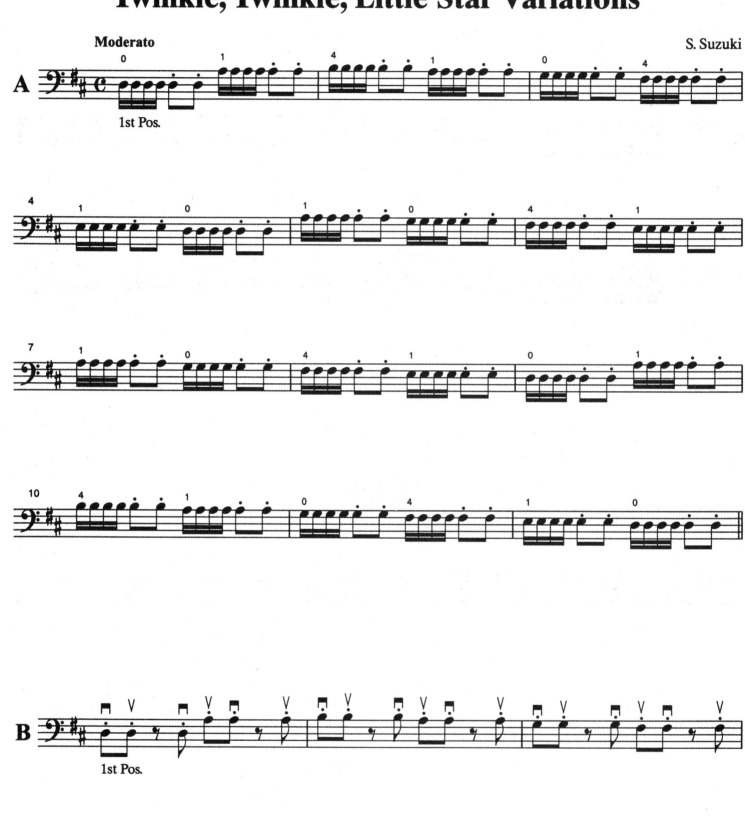

**C**

**D**

**E**

# Theme

Folk Song

## 2
# Go Tell Aunt Rhody

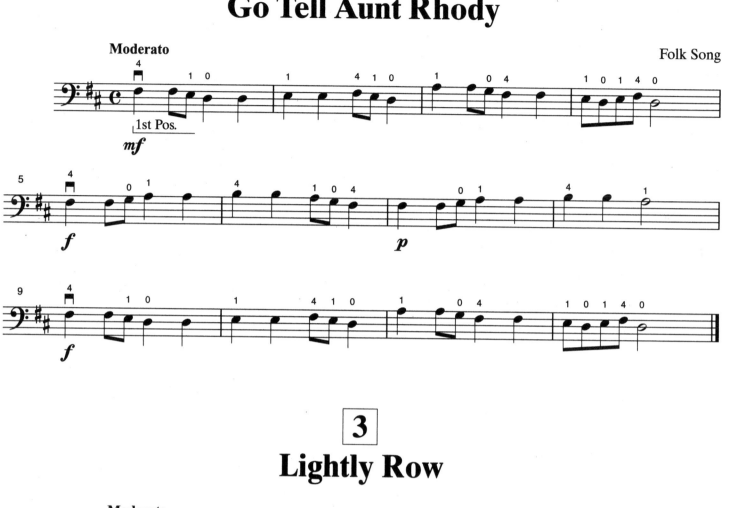

Moderato

Folk Song

## 3
# Lightly Row

Moderato

Folk Song

# Tonalization

4th Pos.

## 4

# Chatter With the Angels

Spiritual

**Moderato**

1st Pos.

*Fine*

4th Pos.

*D.C. al Fine*

14

# 5
# Song of the Wind

Moderato

Folk Song

# 6
# May Song

Allegro moderato

Folk Song

# 7
# French Folk Song

**Moderato**

Folk Song

# 8

# O Come, Little Children

# Bowing preparation for Lament

## Preparation for uneven bowing

# 9
# Lament

# 10
# Perpetual Motion

# 11
# Allegretto

S. Suzuki

1st Pos.

## Variation

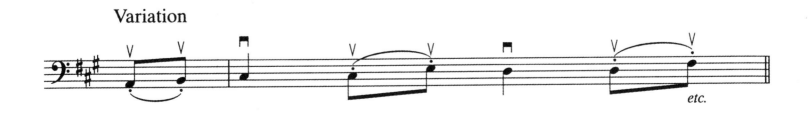

etc.

# 12
# Allegro

S. Suzuki

# 13
# The Little Fiddle

**Allegro**

German Folk Song

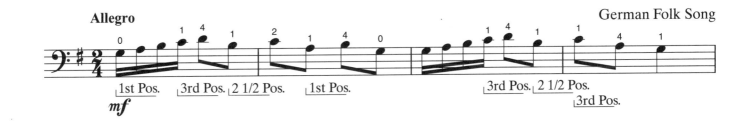

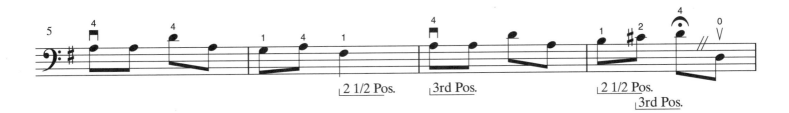